His Light Dispel Your Darkness

Carrie Goodwin

Michael Terence Publishing

First published in paperback by
Michael Terence Publishing in 2020
www.mtp.agency

ISBN 9781800940031

Contents

Synopsis 3

The Lord is My Shepherd 7

Restoration 9

He Guides Me Along the Right Paths for His Namesake 15

Even Though I Walk Through the Darkest Valley 19

I Will Fear No Evil... 25

For You Are With Me, Your Rod & Staff They Comfort Me 27

You Prepare a Table Before Me In The Presence Of My Enemies 35

You Anoint My Head With Oil My Cup Overflows 41

Surely Your Goodness, Mercy & Love Will Follow Me All The Days Of My Life And I Shall Dwell In The House Of The Lord Forever 43

Conclusion 49

Acknowledgements & Bibliography 53

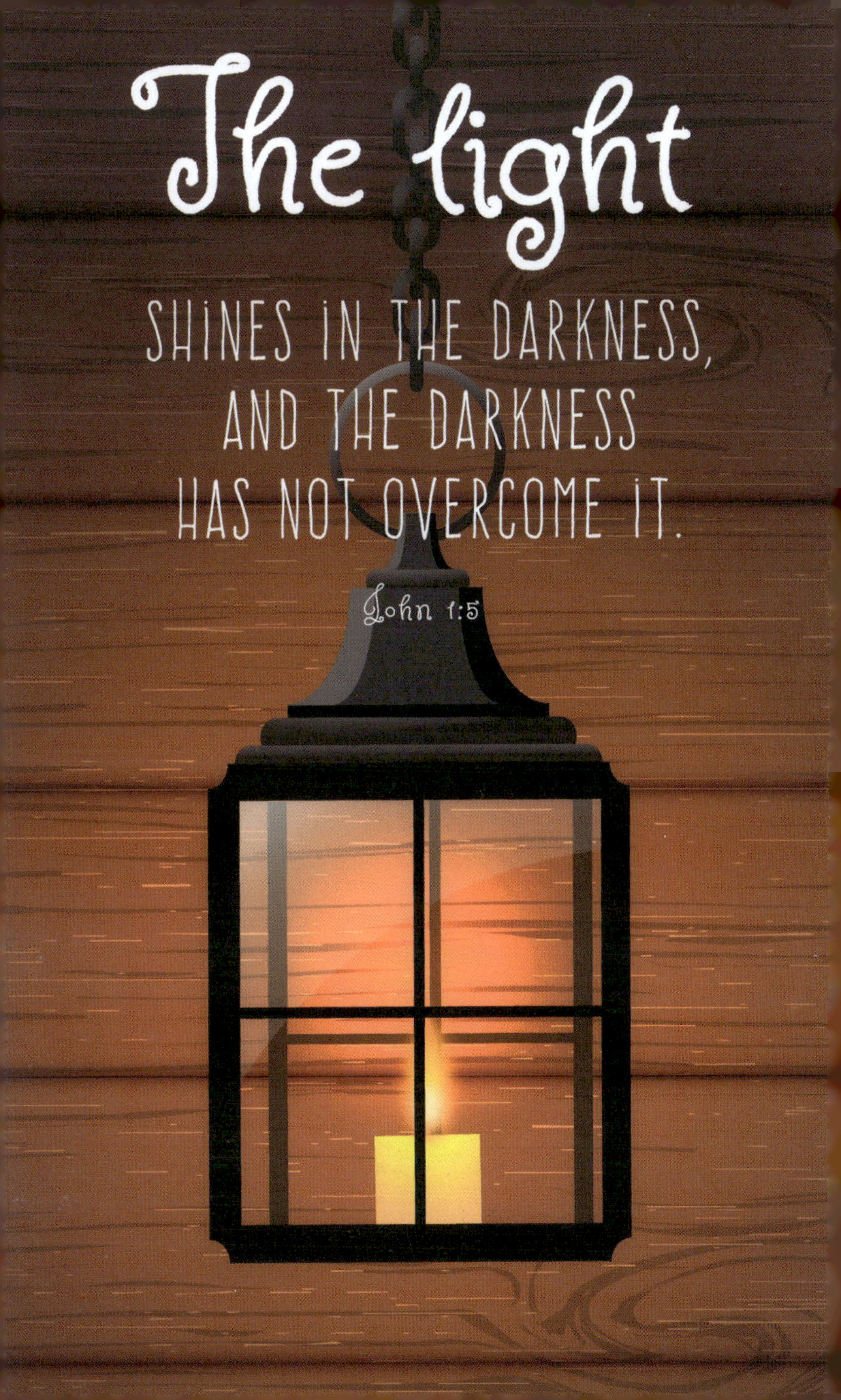
The light
SHINES IN THE DARKNESS,
AND THE DARKNESS
HAS NOT OVERCOME IT.
John 1:5

Synopsis

Can words have the power to promote and heal
So hearts can initiate the magnetic feel
If light is good & darkness bad
Overcome evil overcome sad
The Heavenly realms will Justify
The Lord's mighty word tells how & why

The Lord is My Shepherd

Psalm 23:1-3

The Lord's my Shepherd I shall not want. He makes me lie down in green pastures. He leads me beside still waters he restores my soul.

Restoration

Perseverance strength to endure
A fight so brave eternal cure
Forbearance covers all the earth
To consider the pains of its future birth
With self-control day & night
Away from darkness towards the light
A wave of beauty crystallic sea
Instead of bones & ashes free
Restoring trusting
Eternal peace
Merciful life release
Tender hands a mighty wave
A tune to hear a song to save
Persevere is a trust so bold
Endurance is a fight to the end we're told
The future is a veil
That's waiting to be torn
It rises up
Like the exalting horn

The feel & understanding
Of a patient call
The beauty of truth
Is a claim for all
The sun will shine its healing rays
A joyful hope for future days.

He Guides Me Along the Right Paths for His Namesake

Psalm 23:3

To know the chaos striving strife
Clutching at the straws of life
I will get out of my own way
Shape me mould me I will obey
Maybe I wasn't in control
Have I betrayed you all along?
I give you all I've got to give
Till there's nothing left that's wrong
The tree of life the hedge of fire
To edify the one desire
Gracious Love the restorative kind
Eternal glory seek & find
Can hearts deceive can hearts betray
Purification without delay
The plentiful well the river of life
To turn me away from the valley of woe
Your word is a lamp to guide my feet
It's the only way for us to go

Even Though I Walk Through the Darkest Valley

Psalm 23:4

Weakness is a disease a pathway to sin
Consumes the heart allows it in
Despair & destruction is all that is known
Revenge is the focus folly has flown
To know the mind emotions will
Suppression is a weighty fill
Detrimental unawares
Adverse concealing until it flares
Venturing through the darkest valley
Holding on to vice
Superstitions deadly tricks
An associated price
To reminisce a blackout
Conforming to a lie
Insomnia a sickly bind
It wasn't time to die
Paranoia magnified
Suspicions raised
My hands are tied

The terror is ripe the abyss is real
The stains on the sackcloth
I don't want to feel
The terrors of the night are an endless brawl
I witness my torment I don't want to fall
The conscience creeps a memory glare
Disappointment a gaze aware
Desperation fully known
Knowledge that you're not alone
The vacant blackness
Discerning pain
You carry on but will you gain?
The swaggering & sniffy cuff
To recognize I've had enough
The momentary relapse
The lack of control
Wanting to escape
Seeking parole

I Will Fear No Evil...

How small is the mustard seed
How mighty are the trees
The versatility sustaining life
Creating air & breeze
The humble seed rejoices in hope
As it sets its roots by a stream
The hope can ignite a trust so bold
As it aims to fulfil its dream
A construction of splendour
The power of might
A miraculous radiance
A beaming light
Waiting for nurture
The sun to appear
Embracing the warmth
Nothing to fear

For You Are With Me, Your Rod & Staff They Comfort Me

Psalm 23-4

His grace reveals a restorative kind
Time to dispel a reprobate mind
Spiritual cancer a daily chore
Supernatural insidious war
We don't ask for discipline
But likely it prevails
To realize this must happen
When we let go of the rails
The war is won if you really did try
Conquer sin dispel the lie
The Lord is here to comfort
With his tender loving care
Gentle is the dove heaven in the air
Were reaching for your refuge

Robust & sweet
The king of kings resides in his heavenly seat
My comforter restorer will make me whole
I rejoice I cheer I relay my goal
The fruits of the spirit will surely prevail
I'm a ship in his waters that is free to sail

You Prepare a Table Before Me In The Presence Of My Enemies

Psalm 23:5

To love yourself at a level just right
To honour the needs of an enemy's plight
Saving the love for the close-knit clan
Segregation a worldly plan
Home is considered just bricks & stone
The stigma attached to those alone
Keeping in the comfort zone
Dissensions flare divisions roam
To understand the absent mind
Forget to love
Be cruel or kind
Gossip travels speed of light
The world is small
In times of plight
The colour of mankind
Eternal blend

Anticipate a stranger
Foe or friend
The foes of past will form a line
A truce forgive
A call to dine

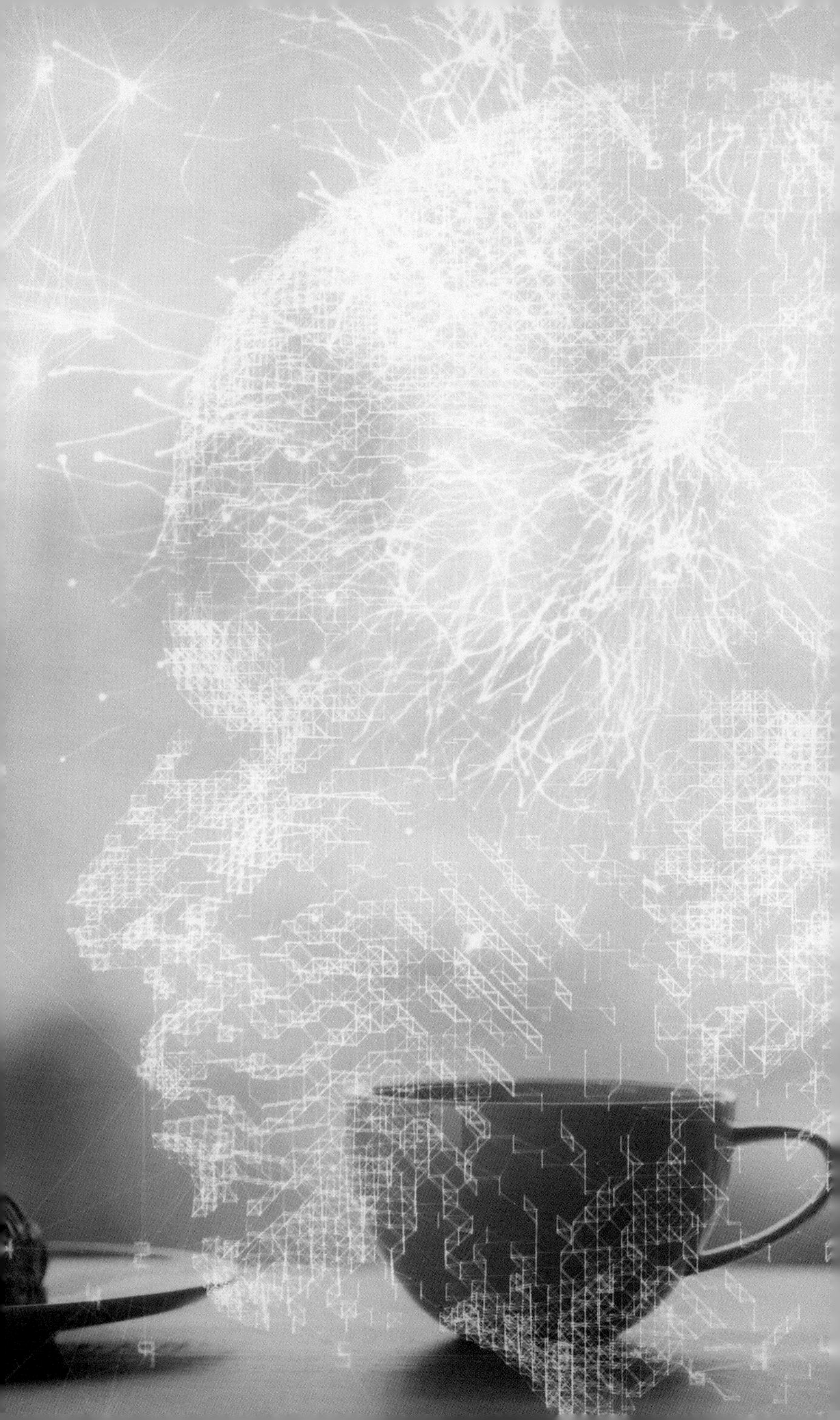

You Anoint My Head With Oil My Cup Overflows

Psalm 23:5

Faith is a shield from the roaming dart
To shine a light that is in our heart
His strength is perfected in our weakness
He increases the power of the listless
Rich in love the power of grace
Priorities we love to face
Hope is a vision of the reality ahead
Nourishes the soul to feed it bread
A humble seed waiting to be sown
The egg cracks & the chick smells home
He's going to lift me & carry me to shore
If I drown I'll be raised like the eagles soar
The truth will appear tis the life & the way
In him we can hope & trust every day
The river of living water will overflow
We can be more than conquerors
At the end of the age we'll know

Surely Your Goodness, Mercy & Love Will Follow Me All The Days Of My Life And I Shall Dwell In The House Of The Lord Forever

Psalm 23:6

His Mercy transcends our comprehension
His Faithfulness the one ascension
We're just wretched blips in his radar
He waits & seeks us from afar
Freedom free to frolic & thrive
Time to explore time to be alive
Protective love embracing peace
Forget the past merciful release
Time to consider a time to shine
Pour on the oil drink new wine
Skipping along with a spring in my stride
No more self-loathing no more pride
Flee the enemy flee from fear
Ears to hear & really hear

Being wise with mourning
Turn it into Joy
Being wise with despair
Turn it into praise
To gently nurture explore the heart
To flourish life & set apart
Important things in life are free
A flower a bird a smile a tree
The heaven's commission
Purpose for the Lord
A mighty Love A mighty sword
He turns the ashes into gold
Beyond the chaos
You will get told
Sin is turned into a song
The transformation
Won't be long

Conclusion

The Lord can pluck us out of our plight
Lead us back towards the light
Take us to a spacious place
Pave the way
Run the race
His mercy love
Sweet embrace
He took an impossible situation
He turned it around
For his glorification

"Break my heart for what breaks yours
Everything I am for your kingdom's cause"

Acknowledgements & Bibliography

My heavenly Father

My Lord Jesus

The Holy Spirit

The Holy Bible – Sword of the Spirit

Hosanna – Hillsong

All the wrong things – Branan Murphy

Printed in Great Britain
by Amazon

57389634R00033